DIVERSIONS
on *the* ROAD *from*
WRITING

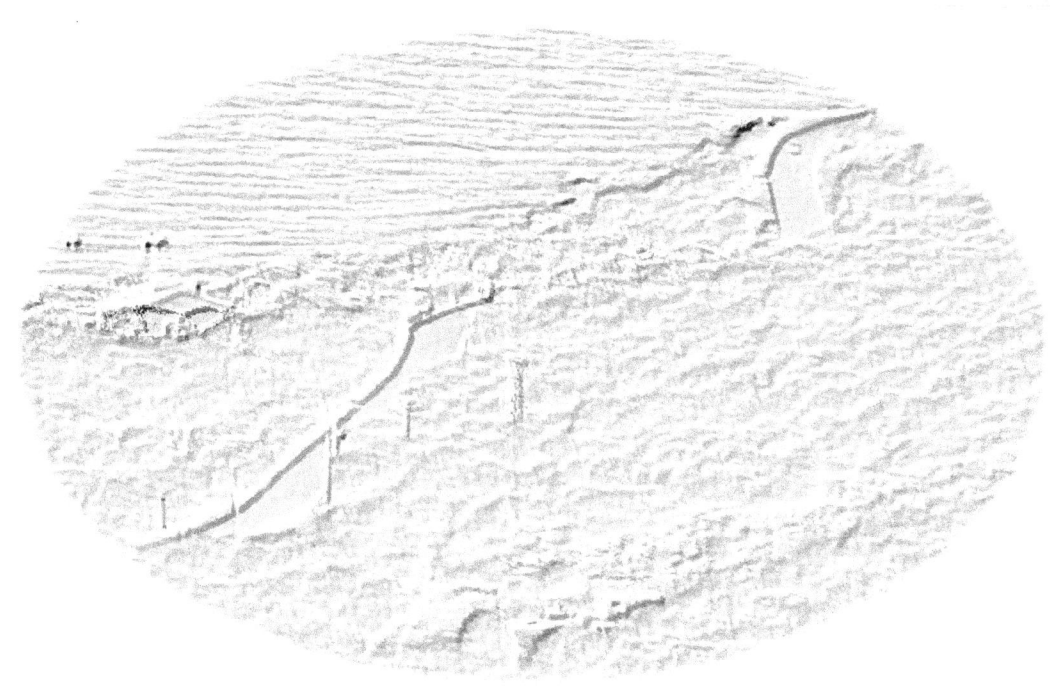

Poems of Pascal Paul Piazza

INK START MEDIA
5710 W Gate City Blvd Ste K #284
Greensboro, NC 27407

INTRODUCTION

I do not publish any work until my work is first vetted. I want to thank, and you may want to blame, Celeste Priest, Bernadette Payne and Neil Backes for reviewing and commenting on these poems.

The draft I submitted for review had footnotes. Published poetry, however, should not have footnotes. Therefore, these poems do not have footnotes.

There are some subjects referenced in the poems that could use some background. Hence, let's discuss some of the issues, ideas or matters that you may have to embrace when reading these poems.

The first poem is very pessimistic. It sets a negative tone. I cannot say that I am divorced from the world that I live in Texas in 2018. I just ask that you wait to the very last poem before making up your mind.

We travel to the outer loops of San Antonio, Texas, even though I live in Houston, Texas. Loop 410 is the inner loop and it is for convenience. Loop 1604 is the outer loop and it is where the city of San Antonio meets the farmlands of Bexar County, Texas and beyond. It's the home of roadside stands selling produce, like the coveted peaches from Fredericksburg, Texas. It is where one can acquire such peaches when I was dispatched on a journey to make up for something stupid I did. Mary DeBauche coined the phrase "apologetic peaches" when I had originally just written peaches. She deserves the credit. Yes, that is the "Mary" of "Mary and Charlotte" fame in the Cycle of Cyrnos: Book One – Origins.

We next hear about five fabulous women who are single and smart and who want to have as little to do with me as they can. It is fun though to try to figure out what my feelings really are for each of them. One of these poems' references Occam's razor (the simplest answer is the correct answer when there are two or more credible options). With most women, Occam's razor does not apply from their standpoint, as there are not two credible options. From my standpoint, I can over-create options and then having the obvious pointed out to me can be helpful.

I saw a billboard about a breakthrough in medicine involving neurons. There was a picture of a neuron in action. Thus, I had to ask about what was going on with the neuron.

That then started a series of one-stanza poems asking questions about famous statements leading to a set of multiple musings about how or why we know. I talk about the first line of Matthew's Gospel, Blaise Pascal's wager that a rational person will wager on the existence of God rather that the opposite because there is so much worse that could happen if God exists and one does not believe, Rene Descartes' pithy "I think therefore I am," and the enigma of parallel lines which lie at the bedrock of geometric reasoning, but which have never been proven to exist.

I want you to read The Immense Journey by Loren Eisley first published in 1946. It is a rational, yet spiritual, guide for anthropologists. It begins with the majesty of nature in its simplest form – water.

We take a step back in time both by going back in time all together and by excavating the past now. We talk about intricate bone and stone carvings that are precise, scientific, artistic and poetic. We then hearken to P. B. Shelley's poem "Ozymandias" and where a Hopewell mound in Ohio provides the focus of attention rather than a decaying statute of an Assyrian ruler.

In a major break, we delve into the philosophy of "carpe diem" which is attributable to the Roman Stoic poet Horace and which was continued by Robert Herrick in his poem "To the Virgins to Make Most of Time" and John Crowe Ransom in his poem "Piazza Piece." We have a conversation between Horace, on one hand, and Herrick and Ransom, on the other end, about whether the Stephen Stills' "love the one you're with" approach adopted by Herrick and Ransom is indeed what Horace meant. Or, did Horace, like other Stoic philosophers like Seneca, champion not letting the future paralyze the present enjoyment of life to the fullest, but tempered by a measured rule with a steady hand of the tiller of the ship of life. I could not resist updating "Piazza Piece" without the flare or grace of the original.

We then explore unrequited love. It is a measure of how futile the language of relationships can be.

We then imagine about a relationship on a vase as we update John Keats poem "Ode on a Grecian Urn."

While we reference classic poems, we invoke Carl Sandberg's poem "Grass" and a generic Kiplingesque poem (with references to Williams Rogers Clark in the Indiana Territory during the American Revolution, the French Foreign Legion veneration of a wooden hand, the geese that saved Rome, and the tireless dedication of, but and lack of respect for our soldiers). In this vein, I could not leave out how to translate or understand Homer. By now, you should realize that I am either strange or crazy.

Which then brings us to a journey in the modern theme-park of the Inferno. Again, I apologize to Dante, but a journey through Hell is a useful literary vehicle.

This is a modern adaptation of the Inferno. As such, some of its past occupants have been allowed to leave as ideas have changed over time.

There is no longer any need for the River Styx or Charon, the ferryman, or the payment of a coin. Our own deeds pave the path to perdition.

The inhabitants of the first level of Dante's Inferno were the great sages of Greece and Rome. There are the Roman Stoics, Horace and Seneca (whom we met earlier), Ovid who wrote the poem "Metamorphoses" as a homage to nature, Archimedes who had his Eureka moment, and Plato and Socrates who are founders of modern philosophy. They were in Hell because they did not know Jesus Christ. That assumed that classical scholars could not follow Christian belief simply and mainly as a matter of timing and not because of the lack of virtue in their lives or teachings. Yet the Word was there from the beginning. Pico della Mirandala and others further showed during the Renaissance that humanism (and its maxim that man was the measure of all things) was not just secular and could be Christian. Humanism was won at the barricades of the American and French Revolutions represented by the Third Estate (or the people). It was also just fun to have some of great minds of Greece and Rome leavening the theme-park.

The main freed occupant, however, is Brutus. Dante believed that the betrayal of Julius Caesar by Brutus meant that he should occupy the lowest level in Hell. Brutus did not betray a friend. He sought to stop the start of tyranny and the end of the Roman Republic. That to me does not merit a life of eternal suffering.

Along the way, we will see references to the Roman poet Virgil who was Dante's guide. There are some twists or turns with references to the fox and crow of Fontaine's Fables, the serpent in the Garden, and a feral hog. There is a reference to the Sirens whose magical voices lured men to their deaths and to the Playboy Mansion with its infamous grottoes. Not to leave the inexplicable out, there is a mention of back-bile which was one of Galen's main humors and which was known by the Latin melan choler from whence we derive the word melancholy (or to Galen the predominance of black bile). Galen's other three main humors gave us the English words sanguine, phlegmatic and choleric or the predominance of blood, phlegm and bile

There are nine (9) levels of Hell. The occupants are as follows:

The folks that give us computer software and cell phones, but with auto-correct that does not listen and that reshapes our words whether we like it or makes repairs without listening and telling us what is going on even though we just told them that something else is going on; Men who abuse love or who are surrounded by women who prefer other women. This is the modern-day Tantalus who is surrounded by such women who he wants but cannot touch;

The myopic who believe there are certain man-made rights, not moral principles, that supersede all else without exception;

Lawyers who inveterately and unreasonably strictly adhere to the original text, who will say whatever they are paid to say, or who have given up;

The anti-science crowd (which is not the sceptic science crowd); Those who seek and gain excess;

Those that abuse the beauty of love and sex; Liars and defamers; and

Those that should stop the liars and defamers, but do not.

There are no persons mentioned by name. If you believe that I am referring to someone in particular, then that means that the person has the attributes of an occupant of Hell – which should give you more pause then to criticize me (although it is always allowed to do so). One of the five women above will tell you that I am always wrong.

I make a less than clever comment that the silver lining to the curiosity of Pandora (the mythological character and not the software) is that we know where hope is – even if it is alone in a box. There is a lesson learned through the trek to Hell which may be revealed in the last poem.

TABLE OF CONTENTS

THE
UNFATHONMABLE
CYNIC

GENESIS CHOICE

God said to you to think and take your place.

You now are the fate of the human race.

We go back to the void with what you know.

Do you start the Big Bang? You say, no!

THE TRULY INEXPLICABLE:

APOLOGETIC LOVE

WHY DO I TRAVEL 1604 RATHER THAN 410?

Some journey to find a promised land,

Others mean to measure mysteries of life,

I search for an apologetic peach; a road-side stand –

A cure for my pride and her heart's strife.

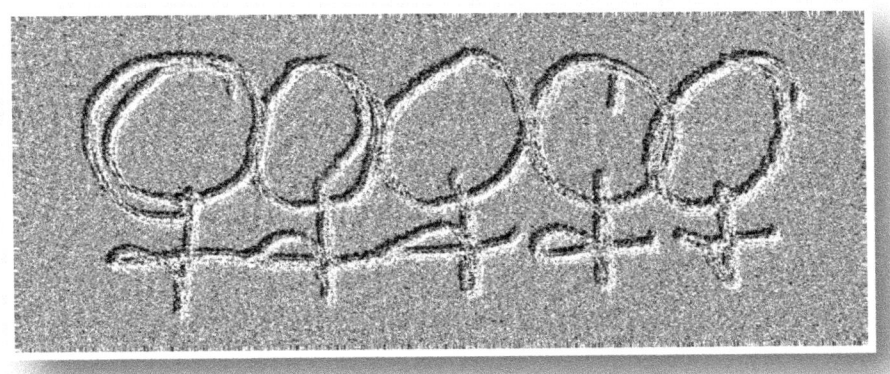

THE INEXPLICABLE -

FIVE WONDERFUL WOMEN

PLE

She is the morning Sun igniting my pace.

She endures trials like no one else with grace.

She is the form that makes a Sun dress flow.

She is the burst sparking the Sun to glow.

DAS

She is Occam's answer to my fictive fear.

Her wry wit matches her curt smirk so clear.

Locks lure for a Venus body and face.

She makes me whole like stars complete dark space.

BP

She is the kiss of elegance and grace.
Urbane, but happy on the Natchez Trace.
Statuesque charms wed with a fiery heart.
Stylish pleasure is reborn with her art.

NA

She is a wild comet in extended flight.

Her orbit is true seeking her own light.

She takes the point, but so often she hides.

She is music and beauty from all sides.

CLP

A constant smile conceals the brightest one.

Two-step master cooking a path to fun.

I am lost to find the end of her charms.

Flaxen hair invites refuge in her arms.

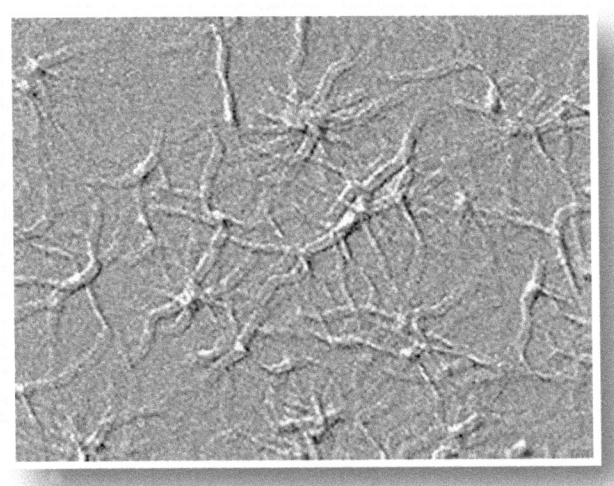

THE UNEXPLAINABLE -

MUSINGS ON
WHAT IF

A neuron snaps a signal unerring

Does it understand what it is saying?

Does it feel the role it is playing?

Does it know or care what it is doing?

The Word was first and the order it brings.

Is it in logic, quarks, quirks and all things?

Or does it watch while life measures its gears?

Is it protean or four thousand years?

The wager is that God is truth and fact.

Only if I care how God may react.

If I find God, is there only one path?

If God is in me, why will there be wrath?

Parallel lines are ninety degrees apart.

Are they, when there is no proof but a heart?

Does it matter if the proof comes out right?

Or a laugh lost within the speed of light.

It is said that I think therefore I am.

Is my heart gone and instinct on the lam?

What is the fate of faith without a clue?

Is this just a mask, as I am blue?

A DISCOURSE OF CREATIVITY

How can you know what we all cannot see?

Easy, there is no end for you or me.

How can you want what we all cannot hear?

Simple, we learn beyond the eye and ear.

Is it real only for our frame of view?

No, the whole draws from many not a few.

Will not a fit-few win the running race?

Not when we join to set a power pace.

Do you make it up to see if it works?

Yes, when proofs produce perpetual perks.

Do the facts guide us to find a right rule?

Maybe, we do not rule out any tight tool.

Is there something which we will never know?

Of course, hubris has its own seeds to sow.

Why not just let God tell us in a Book?

Because, He told us to seek, grow and look!

NO MENUS

As life grew in soup, then it is still that.
Yet, if we say what all is in that vat
the next cook temps flavors not before seen
from the same roux revealing a new scene.

THE AMAZING MAGIC OF NATURE

To Mary at Graduation:

REFLECTIONS ON LOREN EISLEY'S
THE IMMENSE JOURNEY

"If there is magic on this planet,

it is contained in water."

Look, linger. Fluid, flow.

Ripple, restive. Swift, slow.

Humble hum. Cut canyon.

Work wicks. Moist minion.

Sweet source. Launches lives.

Granite grates. Soil survives.

Excited energy. Leaped limit.

Hewn hope. Seized summit.

Congratulations.

Uncle Pascal

LESSONS FROM PREHISTORY

WHAT! YOU DO NOT THINK IT IS POETIC?

A circle that follows the path of the moon
Quarter, half, full, full but not too soon.
A henge that tracks the course of the sun
By lintels and shouldering stones that run.

Any ivory baton narrates a carved bold-bear.
Stones align for a path through there.
A cave forms horses in charcoal and brown.
Flint flakes follow fast both up and down.

Why do you ask that I make each thing
with no written words or runes that ring.
Well, I watch, watch, watch, watch to plan.
I dream, teach, dream. Well, because I can.

ON OZYMANDIAS IN OHIO

There has always been a mound outside the orbit of my town.
Generations glided, gently glanced, going up and then down.
You and I steal away to a secluded side, steeled on a cap cast
by a measured mason of moss and the moist years of Ohio past.

Milk has passed by horse, buggy, truck and the trunk of a car.
Clothes call: buckskin, buckles, flannel, jeans and suits on par.
Yet, the mound anchors solid, still, silent, immutable and late.
For my town, the mound remains a green, grave blank slate.

One morning the earth erupted and my eyes elected to learn
the tale of a trowel tempering the tilled soil with each turn.
The archaeologist now witnessed what he wondered was there.
What we all missed, amused, uncaring, yearly with no care.

The Woodlands culture was restored to life to its earlier day.
A wall of wood watching and marking the moon or sun at play.
He and she stole away on a secluded side; a king wore his best.
The soil surrounds a mirror of who is watching whom at rest.

THE UNFATHONABLE QUESTION -

SEIZE THE DAY
OR WHAT

WHAT DID YOU MEAN HORACE?

Horace heard Ransom and Herrick's hymns
to seize the day with lust above the hems,
as time prefers the rays of a new sun
that warms a path for a race to have fun.

Yes, we should all strike when the iron is hot
with a golden mean and measured plot.
Our ship shifts battered by weathering waves
but sails straight with a firm rudder that saves.

It is now time that we touch the whole cloth
to revive those found with slumber and sloth.
Sow the field, but know the harvest must come
and wider waves flow from the depths we plumb.

There are complements that comprise the whole
where balance bridges the path of the soul.
Wear and tear may linger along with the rust,
but fear is not a better cure than trust.

RETURN TO THE PIAZZA 2013

I am a lady on my cell phone texting,
lounging alone restive in cut-off jeans
cat photos fill both my heart and blank screens.
I see no suitor laughing long or curt.
My heart is now neither happy nor hurt.
There is no rose on my trellis to fade.
The clock on my phone is lost in the shade.
I am a lady on my cell phone texting.

I am the one ready to break the mold.
I may not be who you thought would un-lock
the guard to your heart that abides the clock.
Soon, they will not care for your soul or locks.
But, I always will see outside blocks.
I am a one ready to break the mold.

THE TRULY INEXPLICABLE -

MISSTEPS OF THE HEART

THE RUNNER ON MEMORIAL DRIVE PAUSES ON THE CURB

She stood restive and restless after a run.

A slow stretch immune to the cars.

I see her –

Wow –

I had to brake quickly, but did not stop.

I moved on, as she did, I guess.

I AM STILL CLUELESS

I seek, but fail, to find her hand when we talk
across table-separated chairs in her house.
Her words, contours parry, block and balk.
Her passion still sleeps under that blouse.

I do not know if there are clues in the air,
As we talk for hours and say a lot
Save to know a fantasy in a Stoic stare
a subtle sigh, a naked nape, a sub-plot?

Suddenly, a crack of my wit in a brazen crash;
Is Beatrice at the door in Paradise to enter?
Only to hear laughter and to see the flash
That I still do not know right, left or center.

WHY SHE LEFT ME - I JUST DON'T WANT TO KNOW.

If I look long enough the first flake falls

once again before the winter cold calls.

Flurries cloud without any reason to be.

Eddies make a mirror masking just me.

THE EQUALLY UNEXPLAINABLE -

WHY RUMINATE ON SOME CLASSICS

DESIRES HAVING BEEN DISTRACTED UPON READING "ODE ON A GRECIAN URN"

A muse:

> for my heart to start the beat of a song too long;
> to commit rhyme to time in a line hewn fine.

A poem:

> that rounds the sounds and orders the borders;
> but with no pace or place to rest beneath her breast.

A form:

> Languid in each turn on an urn, so fragile and gracile;
> So much beyond my touch, yet fuse to my muse.

BEFORE THE SNAPSHOT ON THE GRECIAN URN

She and I lay in the open, no care how exposed we are.

Nakedness seems less brazen emboldened in a field afar.

Hand, breast, arm, and leg twist, merge, meander and turn

a double helix releases with two smiles – a picture on an urn.

REFLECTIONS ON
CARL SANDBURG'S "GRASS"

I looked to find a blue-berry among the fields of red

But even plants were covering, out of respect for the dead.

I looked to find an artifact that I could keep for me

But the pieces hid from my sight, so I surely could not see.

I looked to find the battles fought now clouded by the grass

That grows and grows over time in a viscous verdant mass.

I hoped the poem would shed some light to better let me know,

But all I see is more grass, so it is off to war I go.

RESPECT

I am your servant always faithful to my duty.

Water's heart-high waistcoat made us lumber,

Yet we decimated the Albion albatross in slumber.

Our bloody bones have cultivated jungle and sand

With all reminiscences reduced to a wooden hand.

The bridge will be defended with tunics of fleece

Responding to the clarion call of a gaggle of geese.

I am your servant always faithful to my duty.

We are the unknown soldiers with our names.

A postman and an architect live a daily routine

Hiding scars and service and blood in a canteen.

We will re-live the smell of death in any season.

We only ask that our sacrifice has a real reason.

We are the unknown soldiers without names.

ON FAILING TO FIRST LOOK
UPON FAGLES' HOMER

How do I sing the song of Achilles' rage?

With just a quill-pen and words on a page?

I do not know if Achilles used a "k" or a "c"?

Must a line rhyme in order rather than run free?

Keats found in Chapman's Homer the fluid flow

of the depths of the Xanthus in the Decade's show.

I ignore the invitation from Fagles' Homer to see

the epic mirror translates to the modern and me.

I am petulant-proud, sulking along my way,

I boast-hector to fight to keep others at bay.

I crave body-beauty even if I disrespect my host

I am strong-stubborn and covetous for the most.

I know no origins upon whose shoulders I sit,

I am wooden, no guile or horse hewn from wit.

I wander, I travel, along a path with no siren-call.

I judge not, but covet beauty, power, war and all.

I cannot be burdened by chains form the past,

No syllables can change the lot that I have cast.

I find each part of me in the characters so fair

So what if I repeat the mistakes found there!

AN INEXPLICABLE QUEST -

A MODERN JOURNEY TO THE INFERNO

(WITH APOLOGIES TO DANTE ALLEGHERI) 1

I.

WHY I MUST QUEST

I am lost and stuck in this human weir.

I get caught like a fish each time I fear.

I want to jump the dam again to spawn.

But, I school blending to obey each dawn.

I am so lost that I cannot be found.

I see no heart on the path I am bound.

I am a rogue looking to break the mold.

Yet, I am a serf longing to be told.

I know there are guides galore to see.

I find no beacon or compass for me.

I see only buoys with no tether.

I will sink more than float in raw weather.

Someone must have a light to seize the day.

A lamp that measures each wind of the way.

A scale to find the straight and middle.

A level that does not speak by riddle.

Like an epic, my quest sends me to Hell.

I first must fall to know how I may fail.

I will descend starting from the top gate.

I pass nine circles of worsening fate.

II.

THE GATES OF HELL

It is easy to find the gate of woe.
I just need to follow the seeds I sow.
I do not need guile, a guide or a map.
It is a mile, but a narrowing gap.

Concrete invites me as there is no grass.
There are no low or high hurdles to pass.
I see turn-styles like in a theme park.
Tall lights expose and blot out the dark.

Yet, then I was beguiled by three beasts.
A feral hog tempts with signs of full feasts.
A fox has words so sweet to fool a crow.
A snake offers gifts to grow what I will know.

I was about to succumb to each tease.
It took no effort to do so with ease.
Yet, that errand did not fulfill my quest.
I sought to find not my worst but my best.

I took my staff to beat them to gain sway.
But, simple words instead charted my way.
I alone can choose what path I will take.
I can divine what course is real or fake.

III.

WAITING FOR A GUIDE WHO WILL NOT ARRIVE

There is no River Styx to guard the ground.
There is no Charon or boat to be found.
I need no coin for the ferryman's hand.
I have earned my all-day pass to this land.

I had high hopes that a poet would appear
like Virgil did for Dante dispelling fear.
Virgil is gone having left no new guide.
I have no mentor to be by my side.

Horace and Seneca did walk to my side.
Ovid cried asking why nature had died.
Archimedes exclaimed that he then knew.
Socrates and Plato had answers too.

I could not believe that they had left Hell.
I had to know what lesson they would tell.
They had virtues but home was the first ring,
as they did not know what Christ did bring.

Pico found the key so man could measure
to open the door for their long leisure.
Socrates then said that I must learn to ask
why each is there to complete my own task.

III.

THE INHABITANTS HAD CHANGED

The sign said that Brutus had left this place.
He was no longer in the lowest space.
He quickly went from level to level
Following each straight edge, line and bevel.

He was the worst as he cut Caesar's back.
He would suffer, as would his disloyal pack.
Breach of friendship to power was a sin.
He was dispatched to the fiery pin.

But, he did not take lucre or power.
He did not want to build a gold tower.
He was disloyal to excess and vice.
His fealty to truth made him pay the price.

His reprieve came from a rebellious lot.
The sulfur of gun powder made it hot.
The Third Estate rose to pull down the gate.
And broke the locks to Hell albeit late.
The bold barricades wiped his slate clean.
A crown was lost and would never be seen.
No throne would seat the chains that held him.
He no longer battled caprice and whim.

V.

THE FIRST CIRCLE OF HELL

I did not expect to find a valley.

My pulse was quick not letting me dally.

The silicon path gave me two choices:

ones or zeroes in code rather than voices.

I ran into a campus with one door.

I sought to roam the routine on the floor.

I fell in with the mice-men in a maze.

"This is what you want" I heard in a daze.

I did not look like anybody around me.

In a short time, they would have to soon see.

They had their view and I knew I had mine.

We were not the same, like a herd of kine.

I went to speak but I was cut off fast.

My words were wrong and had to be re-cast.

No matter what I said my words were lost.

I could not ask a question at any cost.

My quest quaked stumbling with a false start.

Where is an answer in whole or in part?

What can I learn from a path that is closed?

Do not reshape the question that is posed.

VI.

THE SECOND CIRCLE OF HELL

I stumbled onto well-kept and green grounds.
There was a mansion with clear Siren sounds
I saw pools that led me to a grotto.
Maybe I had left Hell and won some lotto.

My leer saw women beyond my own dreams.
They sat and stood on crests and in soft seams.
Auburn and brown hair fell on naked napes.
Lurid, languid legs lift from satin drapes.

A man went by like the women were not there.
How could he bypass with less than a care?
I said, "why do you walk and do not touch?
I do not know why you could miss so much?"

He said, "you know my father from his past.
His hand could not grasp food or drink to last.
My lust consumed love for my pain and strife.
They love each other, but not me, for life."

I knew that I could be like him with lust.
I too had lost a core respect and trust.
Passion excels over excess that is wrong.
It is balance that makes all of us strong.

VII.

THE THIRD CIRCLE OF HELL

I saw Charon trolling among the brown yards.

He found cold coins from broken jars and shards.

No one was there to attend to the land.

Broken things lay about on gravelly sand.

"What are you doing?" I asked him in jest.

He said that he craved coins for his chest.

But no one needed him to ferry the Styx.

So he went to each circle to find picks.

He said, "look, each house has only one door.

They walk away with no meeting in store.

No one has talked to the other for years.

They found it easy just to make up fears.

One house says it is my land go away.

One lauds that I am immune if I pray

One yells not to take my gun from my hand.

One says that everyone must join my band."

There are absolutes that cannot be denied.

But not ideas that refuse to be tried.

The design tells us to tend to the vine.

There is nothing about acting like kine.

VIII.

THE FOURTH CIRCLE OF HELL

I found a parchment with a hoary past.
A text from Horace may end my flight fast.
But, how do I know what key may be found?
I can ask three counsels caught in the round.

The first was stout and lived in the shade.
"We have to look to the intent when made.
What it may mean to us does not matter.
So seize the day and live and be fatter."

The next was opaque with no guilt to feel.
"We want to attack the text with full zeal.
We do not ask what is right, wrong or true.
For a fee, it means what it means to you."

The third was thin and asleep on a rock.
"Why do you care to know or take stock?
The system is slow and hopes you settle.
Asking for truth only means you mettle."

I can read without the help of a sage.
Horace spoke of the future on each page.
We are all a part of a golden mean.
So I strike sloth with the truth that I glean.

IX.

THE FIFTH CIRCLE OF HELL

So far, I still searched for my marker.

When I heard sounds like a circus barker.

"There is but one way to find a true path.

Look for the one set course among the wrath."

"There is a demon that is worse than all.

It is a curse that fuels a faithful fall.

We must go to war now not to fall down.

We must long escape from a sewer town."

"It says that we make the climate change.

Yet, heat follows its own cycle and range.

We are too small to impact the Grand Plan.

We create culture only for our clan."

"They want to inject disease to save us.

We are to have the pox to stop the pus.

Our cells fight on their own without a drug.

We do not succumb to their mutant bug."

But, I cannot avoid what I can see.

I will test to know and learn to be free.

Wisdom is just science and faith as one.

This is a detour of doubt that is done.

X.

THE SIXTH CIRCLE OF HELL

Steam felt good as it enveloped my face.
Then, the humid heat hit hard like a mace.
I sank into a bog pit a mile down.
My cheeks blushed red and white like a clown.

Magma wands wicked making the floor hot.
Water trickled down to boil on the spot.
It scalded hands, backs and legs of the few
caught up to their necks in this steamy stew.

A bubble held me from the jungle heat.
It supplied me with a protected seat.
I could hear the screams of pain and despair.
They did not want me to forget them there.

"We had boats, cars and gold beyond compare.
We had more than we wanted in our lair.
We were the one percent sharing the wealth.
We said we will share once, but that was stealth."

Just because one can does not mean one should.
Take the chance to do what you will and could.
There is no gain resulting from such excess.
But I still have not found the key to success.

XI.

THE SEVENTH CIRCLE OF HELL

Fire and brimstone do exist in fact.
Beneath the magma there was a hot tract.
Skin did fry and cries did bounce off the roof.
The pain of perdition had its perfect proof.

Excess knows no bounds, color, hue or shape.
Sex is not pleasure when it becomes rape.
Anger is balance 'til consumed by rage.
Self-belief informs 'til it takes the stage.

Profit does not employ and build with greed.
There is no case to want others to bleed.
A breast is not a joy when there is lust.
Food is pain when it oozes to the dust.

Before me are those that ignored these rules.
They jumped the path-edge like stubborn mules.
It was easy to reward their own lust.
It was such pleasure to do as they must.

Tongues, now dry, taste the bitter and sour.
Cracked lips sear on ash each long hour.
They were exposed to be fed on by the birds.
Pointless pain taught me with no need for words.

XII.

THE EIGHTH CIRCLE OF HELL

The fifty columns once held up the light.
A beacon on the hill for those in flight.
They are but strewn stone shambles in a heap.
It does appear that we sow what we reap.

He chose, but did not have, to make them fall.
He had the power to make them rise tall.
He had them broken as a part of a game.
He could now create someone else to blame.

He lay in ruins with acid burning him.
All of his insults scorch and sear his whim.
His eyes do not see what he has just done.
Because he has not lost, but he has won.

His bile swells to invoke prayer and pride.
He laughs as both lay dying at his side.
He does not care as long as he looks good.
And we talk just about him all we could.

He tweets a lie is truth and truth are a lie.
Lies crush his soul like a pea in a die.
Moral fiber burns like straw in a blaze.
He fiddles as he sees all that he can raze.

XIII.

THE NINTH CIRCLE OF HELL

There are souls worse than the lustful liars.
It is a nest now lost in the pit-fires.
I walk down to find a small teaming host.
Their fetid flesh doomed to suffer most.

There was a horror that they all well knew.
The tweets targeted all but a rare few.
There was no humor other than black bile.
Caprice wed disrespect as a new style.

There are moments to mark a person's life.
One can elevate or succumb to strife.
Our acts must exceed odds or blind fealty.
A moral compass finds higher realty.

They failed each test missing the main mark.
The dark killed the light with no new spark.
Now, what is fake is real and false is true.
Fear, hate and lust define red, white and blue.

They gutted duties that measure us all.
A bold betrayal that fostered their fall.
They suffer just as they chose not to act.
Acute pain scores when they did not react.

XIV.

THE RETURN

I have seen the worst that evil can be.

That sight weighs a heavy burden on me.

Yet, I rise hand over hand on the rope.

Not to hang my head, but to tether hope.

This trek has ended so I resume life.

I repel up waiting for peace and strife.

I will bang my head against many walls.

I will elevate to avoid the falls

I must not betray the duties I owe.

That is the great gift my journey did show

Each of us look to a different source.

Whether God, nature or a designed course.

My measure is not man or a terse tweet.

Raising dignity is the goal to meet.

That applies to me, right, left, rich and poor.

I embrace you, science, faith, facts, love and lore.

I reject the blind iron mask of fear.

Derision and hate will have no place here.

I may dissent, but I will use your name.

I will look up to smile and learn just the same.

XV.

EPILOGUE

I am still enmeshed with questions and trials.

I will face the pressure of pressing piles.

Yet, knowing the integrity of my path,

I will drink wine not the grapes of wrath.

I will fail and falter more times than not.

It is easy to collapse on the spot.

But the black clouds do not have to mean rain.

They are comfort to seek to salve the pain.

It may look like there is no hope in sight.

The fake may appear to win over right.

There is reason not to doubt or to fear.

Diligence as vigilance remains clear.

I may now want to strike out and to hit.

A blood rush quickens the race to a fit.

A short rush does not build or grow a thing.

Finding the good always sponsors a fling.

I know that the world has not changed much.

Pandora left hope in the box as such.

But, we know where hope lives and can be found.

There are smiles and reason to go around.

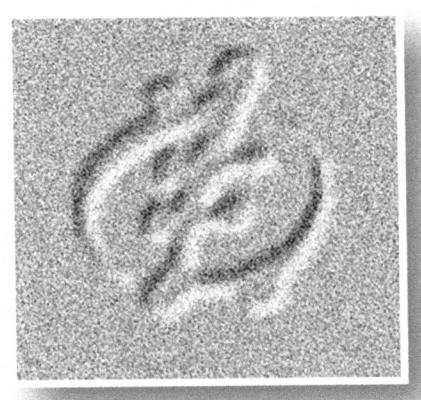

THE UNFATHOMABLE OPTIMIST -
RETURN TO THE
BEGINNING

GENESIS CHOICE REDUX

God said to you to think and take your place.

You now are the fate of the human race.

In the void, flux-time seeds a guess and mess.

Do you start the Big Bang? You say, yes!